First published in 2010 as *Betong – en gjuten hobby* by Sania Hedengren and Susanna Zacke, Bokförlaget Semic, Sundbyberg, Sweden

Photography by Anna Skoog
Graphic design by Marianne Lilliér

Skyhorse Publishing books may be purchased in bulk at special discounts for sales promotion, corporate gifts, fund-raising, or educational purposes. Special editions can also be created to specifications. For details, contact the Special Sales Department, Skyhorse Publishing, 307 West 36th Street, 11th Floor, New York, NY 10018 or info@skyhorsepublishing.com.

Skyhorse® and Skyhorse Publishing® are registered trademarks of Skyhorse Publishing, Inc.®, a Delaware corporation.

www.skyhorsepublishing.com

10 9 8 7 6 5 4 3 2 1

Library of Congress Cataloging-in-Publication Data

Hedengren, Sania.
  [Betong en gjuten hobby. English]
  Concrete crafts : simple projects from jewelry to place settings, birdbaths to umbrella stands / Sania Hedengren & Susanna Zacke photography Anna Skoog ; translated by Anette Cantagallo.
        pages cm
  "First published in 2010 as Betong en gjuten hobby by Sania Hedengren and Susanna Zacke, Bokforlaget Semic, Sundbyberg, Sweden."
  ISBN 978-1-62636-544-5
  1. Handicraft. 2. House furnishings. 3. Garden ornaments and furniture—Design and construction. 4. Concrete. I. Zacke, Susanna. II. Title.
  TT910.H4313 2014
  745.5—dc23
                              2013033321

Printed in China

Concrete Crafts

Simple Projects from Jewelry to Place Settings, Birdbaths to Umbrella Stands

Sania Hedengren & Susanna Zacke

Photography Anna Skoog

Translated by Anette Cantagallo

SKYHORSE PUBLISHING

Contents

Concrete: An Awesome Material!

It's finally done: *Concrete Crafts,* the book we thought was missing from the shelves. We want to share our ideas about concrete and the joys of crafting with it. Casting your own creations isn't difficult, and you can make your own professional-looking concrete decorations and furniture in as little as one day.

Mix fine concrete with water and pour into molds of various shapes. Once it's dried, remove the concrete from the mold, and you're done! Our experience has taught us that once you've started and finished your first small project—which can be as simple as pouring concrete into an old plastic container and dropping in a tea light—the ideas will start flowing. Concrete is such a versatile, awesome material that it's difficult to stop once you've started!

The key is to find sturdy, interesting, and whimsical molds to cast in. These can be common plastic bowls, barrels, buckets, or old plastic containers. For example, a toilet brush holder molds a perfect candy bowl; a plastic bottle cut in half makes an adorable candleholder; and crocheted fabric creates beautiful patterns on bowls. The list goes on. . . .

In this book you will find some thirty projects, and while we tried to divide these projects into themes, the versatile nature of concrete means that these projects can't always be put into categories. They are all, however, fun, stylish, practical, and decorative. These items have hundreds of uses, both indoors and out!

We hope you'll appreciate the wide variety of ideas as you turn from one page (which might explain how to cast a barbecue stand) to the next (which can show how to cast small decorative birds in ice cube trays . . .).

Learn, be inspired, and then head out to get a bag of concrete and a few buckets and molds, and start creating.
GOOD LUCK!

Sania and Susanna

Good to Know

WHAT IS CONCRETE?

Concrete consists of 80 percent ballast rock, which is comprised of sand, stone, and gravel. Fourteen percent is cement, which consists of heated and ground limestone, and 6 percent is water. Concrete is therefore a natural material that is eco-friendly, useful, and long lasting.

Concrete is also one of the world's most important building materials, and it has a long history in the construction industry. There are very old structures, such as amphitheaters, bridges, and houses, that are made of concrete, and they have stood for thousands of years.

The fine concrete that we've used for the projects in this book will be relatively smooth because it's made of tiny stones, about an eighth of an inch in size. If you want it to be even smoother, you can use a concrete mix used in repairs; you can find all kinds of concrete at your local home improvement store.

MOLDS

The shape you cast in is the most important part of the process, as it's the part that delivers the results. It's here that you have to use your imagination. Plastic is a good material because it's elastic and has a smooth surface that won't stick to the concrete. However, many other materials, such as heavy cardboard, wood, and metal, also work just fine. Remember to brush the inside of the mold with vegetable oil to loosen the concrete from the sides.

Buckets, sandbox toys, plastic bowls, tubs, bottles, and old packaging are all examples of good, inexpensive molds that you can use to make pots, birdbaths, candleholders, and more.

For tabletops, benches, and shelves, you'll need to build your own shape using particle board and formworks. You can also look around at flea markets and thrift stores for inexpensive options and whimsical shapes. It can even be as simple as using ice cube trays from Ikea. Sometimes in order to remove the set concrete, you'll have to cut the mold, so it makes sense to use an old plastic container that would have gone to waste anyway.

REINFORCEMENT

Reinforcing the concrete is necessary when you cast larger pieces. For example, a tabletop must be strengthened to keep it from breaking. The reinforcement also makes the concrete more resistant to frost. To reinforce concrete, use rebar, reinforcement mesh, hardware cloth, or chicken wire. We use chicken wire for our projects, because the wire is soft and can be easily cut with a pair of pliers.

To use chicken wire as reinforcement, trim a piece of wire to fit the mold. Push the wire down into the wet concrete, and cover with a little more concrete to keep the mesh in place. It's not nearly as complicated as it may sound. You can read more about this in each project.

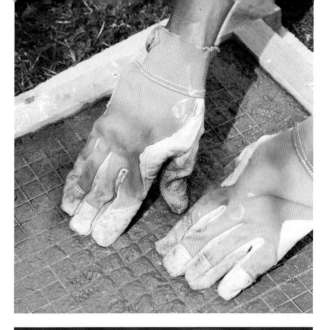

DECORATION

To give the concrete that extra touch, you can decorate it with a variety of different things. A pot, for example, can be decorated with mosaic pieces that you press down into the wet concrete.

If you want your mosaic to have an irregular pattern, you can break old chipped porcelain and freely mix the different patterns and colors. People often sell their old crockery at garage sales, and you can usually get it quite cheap. You can also buy odd, single tiles or cheap mosaic pieces from a tile store.

Natural materials, such as beautiful stones or seashells, also add a nice decorative touch. A variation on this theme is to cast the decoration itself. For example, you can make thin sheets of concrete that you can then attach to the birdbath or the bowl, or why not decorate

concrete also works really well and creates a really pretty effect.

WAITING TIME

When the concrete is "curing," it refers to the process of drying, hardening, and solidifying. The length of time will vary depending on the thickness and size of what you cast, but expect to wait at least twenty-four to forty-eight hours.

When it cures, cover the concrete object well with plastic; a bag, tarp, or plastic sheeting is fine to use. Put the object in a cool and shady place. To make the concrete cure more slowly, use a spray bottle to spray it with water a few times while it is curing.

It takes a lot of patience to wait for the concrete to dry; we know. You just get so curious. But try not to remove the piece too early, or else you risk breaking it. Be patient and wait the recommended twenty-four hours.

with that little figurine you cast in the ice cube tray? If you'd like to make a pattern embedded in the concrete (when making a bowl or something similar), simply line the bottom of the mold with a crocheted fabric. Ceiling roses can also add nice patterns to trays or medallions; there's more on this later in the book. Painting on

It takes a lot of patience to
wait for the concrete to cure;
we know.

Mixing Concrete

The first step when you begin casting in concrete is, of course, to mix the concrete. To make the mix, you only really need to combine water and fine concrete.

Here's a list of materials you'll need and a description of what to do with them. These descriptions apply to any project you might make with concrete casting.

THE MATERIALS & TOOLS YOU NEED

- Fifty-five pound bags of fine concrete that you can buy in home improvement stores.
- One or two regular plastic buckets to mix in.
- Water.
- A spade or trowel to stir with. You can also get a mixing paddle attachment for a drill, so your arms don't get so tired. You can find this kind of paddle at the home improvement store. If you are going to mix a large amount of cement and want to invest in a cement mixer, you can find these in home improvement stores, too; however, they cost upward of several hundred dollars, so renting might also be a good option.
- Gloves. Make a habit of using gloves, since the concrete mixture is corrosive and dries the skin.
- Mask. Don't breathe the dust from the dry concrete! Use a facemask for protection.

A STARTING TIP:

"Have all the molds you intend to use prepared and ready before you mix the concrete."

Start by pouring a drop of water into the bucket. Then pour in the concrete powder (measurements can be found on the packaging). With practice, it's quite easy to mix concrete "by feel," which can be easier if you are not mixing a lot. Stir, blend, and mix very thoroughly with a spade or mixing paddle. If you are mixing a whole bucket, a mixing paddle is recommended. The consistency of the concrete should resemble thick porridge. Making concrete is that simple.

To specify the exact amount of concrete needed for the various projects is impossible because it depends entirely on what is to be cast and the size of the individual mold. A bucket of mixed concrete is enough to make about two regular-sized pots.

Mix the concrete as you pour, one bucket at a time. You shouldn't let the concrete mix stand for too long as it will begin to cure and harden.

Clean the tools and equipment immediately, as it may be impossible to remove the concrete once it has hardened. Keep a bucket of water or a garden hose handy.

In a bucket or something similar, mix the fine concrete with water.

A mixing paddle attached to a drill or electric screwdriver eases the mixing. You can mix by hand, although the concrete is a bit heavy.

Of course, it's best to work outdoors in the garden, because concrete can be messy. But if you don't have a garden, that doesn't mean you should refrain from casting. The balcony is also a great option. In the winter it is too cold to do concrete casting outdoors as the wet concrete cannot handle freezing temperatures. So, if you want to cast an advent candleholder for Christmas, it's a good idea to stay inside—just make sure to cover the table or the floor completely, and pour the fine concrete gently to keep the dust from spreading. And stick to smaller projects.

LET'S GET STARTED!

Rhubarb Leaf FRUIT BOWL

Let's start with a real classic that's worth repeating! Begin by picking a large, robust, and beautiful rhubarb leaf.

- Form a mound of earth or sand and place the rhubarb leaf on top, "face" down. For convenience, we formed our mound in a tub; a wheelbarrow or a children's sandbox works great, too!
- Mix the concrete as described on page 12.
- Apply the concrete to the top of the leaf.
- Spread the concrete so that it covers the entire rhubarb leaf, and be sure to align the edges.
- Flatten the center so that the bowl will stand upright and stable when finished.
- Let the concrete cure and dry for at least twenty-four hours. Don't place it in direct sunlight.
- For best results, you can spray the concrete with water a few times during the drying period.
- Once the concrete has finished curing, carefully remove the leaf.
- The bowl is now ready. It's just as beautiful outside in the garden as it is on the table inside.

Form a mound of earth and place the upside-down rhubarb leaf on top.

Apply the concrete on top of the leaf. Spread the concrete to cover the entire leaf and make sure to align the edges.

14

The bowl with the beautifully engraved leaf veins is now ready to be placed on the table.

Instead of Ice . . .

Here's one of our easiest concrete crafts. It's a perfect project for casting with the kids! This project uses an ice cube tray—Ikea usually has whimsical ice cube trays in the shape of different figures. So what do you do with concrete figurines, one wonders? Well, next time a friend invites you over for drinks, why not give your host a pair of happy concrete duckies instead of a boring flower bouquet?

- Apply vegetable oil to the inside of the mold.
- Mix the concrete as described on page 12.
- Fill the mold with concrete.
- Gently tap the mold against the ground a few times to remove any air bubbles.
- Let the concrete cure and dry for least twenty-four hours. Don't place it in direct sunlight.
- For best results, you can spray the concrete with water a few times as it dries.
- Carefully remove the figures from the mold.
- Now you have a little flock of duckies!

The ice cube tray has been filled with concrete instead of water, and it will now cure for twenty-fours.

These adorable little duckies lined up in a row make for delightful window decorations.

A little concrete duckie can decorate the dining table.

CONCRETE *Napkin Weight*

It's time to bring out your inner child, as well as the sandbox toys! A regular sandbox toy is the perfect mold to cast in. This concrete turtle is a great paperweight for napkins.

- Apply vegetable oil to the inside of the mold.
- Place a pretty bead, stone, or gem at the bottom of the mold for a touch of color.
- Mix the concrete as described on page 12.
- Fill the mold with concrete.
- Gently tap the mold on the table or the ground to remove any air bubbles.
- Let concrete cure and dry for at least twenty-four hours. Don't place it in direct sunlight.
- For best results, spray the concrete with water a few times during the drying period.
- Loosen the figure from the mold.

After placing a stone or gem at the bottom, fill the mold with concrete.

Look how cute the little concrete turtle is!

Tabletop WITH A TILE PLATE

Furniture can also be cast in concrete. A tabletop is relatively simple to make, and when it's finished, you can just attach it to a table base or legs. First build a mold, and then reinforce it with chicken wire to keep the tabletop sturdy. A beautifully patterned tile set in the middle of the tabletop becomes the icing on the cake.

- This mold is made out of particle board and a standard formwork that you can find at the lumberyard.
- Measure and screw the bolts to the desired dimensions.
- Screw the formwork into the particle board.
- Cut the chicken wire to fit inside the mold.
- Mix the concrete as described on page 12.
- Place an ornate tile facing down in the mold.
- Pour in the concrete.
- Press the chicken wire into the concrete.
- Gently tap the mold on the ground a few times to remove any air bubbles from the concrete.
- Let the concrete slab cure and dry for at least twenty-four hours. Don't place it in direct sunlight.
- Spray the concrete with water a few times during the drying period.
- Carefully pry the finished tabletop from the mold.
- Either attach the slab to a chassis or screw the legs on. Now you have a wonderful garden table!

The rough concrete surface contrasts beautifully with the colorfully patterned tile plate.

"We like to divide the garden into small sections, each with its own theme and unique purpose. Concrete comes in handy everywhere. The barbeque corner with the grill, the arbor with the garden table, the walkway with the pretty concrete slabs, the greenhouse with the concrete steps, and the flowerbed with the concrete pots—unleash your imagination!"

The mold is built from particle board and a standard formwork. We made two tabletops at the same time, one right next to the other. Measure and screw the formwork to the desired shape and screw it onto the particle board.

Place a tile upside down in the mold.

Pour the concrete into the mold, and press the reinforcement into the wet concrete.

*Your own personalized table is done!
It's perfectly suited for coffee breaks
in the garden.*

Hello!

A delightful welcome sign with the word "Hello" is a nice detail to place at the entrance to your garden. In our Swedish home, we've used our native "Hej" to greet our friends. Wooden letters are available at the local craft store, so your sign can say whatever you want!

Build a mold from a formwork and particle board, and lay the letters in the bottom of the mold. Keep in mind that they must be backward to you. To make the sign durable, it should be reinforced, but if it's not too big or weight bearing, reinforcement won't be needed.

"Sometimes projects don't turn out as planned! It happens to everyone—even us. The concrete can crack, contain air bubbles, get stuck in the mold. . . . Don't get discouraged, and learn from your mistakes, just like we've done many times."

- The mold is made from particle board and a standard formwork that can be found at the lumberyard.
- Measure and screw the formwork into the desired shape.
- Screw the formwork onto the particle board.
- Place the letters backward on the particle board and nail them into the board to secure them.
- If you are using chicken wire as reinforcement, cut it to fit the mold.
- Mix the concrete as described on page 12.
- Pour the concrete into the mold.
- Press the chicken wire into the concrete.
- Gently tap the mold against the ground a few times to remove any air bubbles.
- Let the sign cure and dry for at least twenty-four hours. Don't place it in direct sunlight.
- For best results, spray the concrete with water a few times during the drying period.
- Gently bend the mold to remove the sign.
- Now the sign is done and you can display it anywhere, inside or out!

Build the mold from particle board and a formwork. Letters from your local craft store create a word written in concrete.

Lay the letters flat so the word is backward to you, and nail them securely into the board.

Fill the mold with concrete.

Plate HOLDER

After a trip to the flea market, we came home with a beautiful old porcelain plate and thought it would make a perfect concrete project. We cast the plate in a drum of concrete and it now sits in the garden as a decoration.

- Choose a plastic tub to make the drum (we used a rounded shape).
- Apply vegetable oil to the inside of the tub.
- Mix the concrete as described on page 12.
- Pour concrete into the tub, but don't fill it up all the way. There should be space for the plate.
- Push the plate into the wet concrete.
- Weigh the plate down with a few large stones.
- Allow the drum to cure and dry for at least twenty-four hours. Don't place it in direct sunlight.
- Spray the concrete with water a few times during the drying period.
- Remove the weights and remove the concrete from the tub.
- The concrete plate holder is now ready to use as a birdbath, a decoration—you name it!

A beautiful old plate from the flea market.

The tub has been filled with concrete, and the plate was pushed down into it; some heavy rocks hold the plate in place while the concrete dries.

" Visiting the flea market is one of our favorite things to do. When you find a great bargain it feels like you've found buried treasure. Whether you pick up something that's good to use on its own, or that you know you want to restore, wash, grind down, rebuild, or fix, it's all just as exciting! "

A Charming Bowl

This lovely dish was molded in a somewhat large plastic bowl. The pattern was created using a crocheted fabric. You can usually find cheap, crocheted tablecloths at flea markets and secondhand shops. Buy them as you find them, so you have a small stock in various shapes and sizes.

- Turn the plastic bowl upside down and place the crocheted fabric on top.
- Apply vegetable oil to the surface (on both the bowl and the cloth).
- Mix the concrete as described on page 12.
- Cover the bowl and cloth with the concrete. Spread it so the entire surface of the bowl is covered by an even layer—about ½ to ¾ of an inch (1–2 cm) thick.
- Let the bowl cure and dry for at least twenty-four hours. Don't place it in direct sunlight.
- For best results, spray the concrete with water a few times during the drying period.
- Carefully remove the concrete from the plastic bowl and pull off the cloth.
- The bowl is now ready for use.

Turn the plastic bowl upside down and place the cloth on top. The cloth will create a pretty pattern on the inside of the concrete bowl.

Cover the surface with a layer of concrete, about ½ to ¾ of an inch (1–2 cm) thick.

An absolutely charming bowl for fruit, vegetables, chips—whatever you want.

Kitchen SHELVES

Kitchen shelves on brackets are a nice alternative (or a great complement) to cabinets.
We made this shelf out of concrete, and to make the slab extra smooth, it was cast on a glass plate. This makes the concrete almost as smooth as a mirror. If you don't have any sheets of glass, this step can, of course, be excluded, but we wanted to show you how to do it anyway.

- Build the mold for the shelf with particle board and a standard formwork. These can be purchased at the lumberyard.
- Measure and screw the formwork into the desired shape.
- Screw the formwork onto the particle board.
- Order a sheet of glass with the same measurements as the inside dimensions of the mold. This can be obtained from a glazier or home improvement store.
- Place the glass on the particle board, inside the frame.
- Brush the glass thoroughly with vegetable oil.
- For reinforcement, cut chicken wire to fit the mold.
- Mix the concrete as described on page 12.
- Pour the concrete on top of the glass plate until the mold is full.
- Press the chicken wire into the wet concrete.
- Gently tap the mold against the ground a few times to remove any air bubbles.
- Let the concrete cure and dry for at least twenty-four hours. Don't place it in direct sunlight.
- Spray the concrete with water a few times during the drying period.
- Carefully remove the shelf from the mold and the glass plate.
- The shelf is ready to be set into place on brackets.

Place a sheet of glass into the mold to give the shelf a smooth surface.

The mold is filled with concrete, covering the glass plate. We made two shelves at the same time, one right next to the other.

The shelf is in place, on the brackets, in the kitchen.

The shelf surface is extra smooth and fine, because it was cast on a glass plate.

Adorable JEWELRY

You can easily make custom necklaces with a piece of modeling clay and a tiny splash of concrete. We recommend you use a more fine-grained concrete. To make a mold, use clay and a blunt paintbrush handle. Thread the jewelry with a beautiful ribbon. Now you've got a personal piece to wear with pride!

- To make a mold, use model clay from the craft or toy store.
- Press a pattern into the clay with a blunt paintbrush handle or something similar. We made a flower shape.
- Insert a toothpick where you want the hole for threading the ribbon.
- Mix the concrete as described on page 12.
- Fill the mold with concrete.
- Let the jewelry cure and dry for at least twenty-four hours. Don't place it in direct sunlight.
- Spray the concrete with water a few times during the drying period.
- Carefully remove the jewelry from the mold and thread it with either cotton thread or a thin metal wire. Shape it into a loop and attach it to a band, chain, or thin leather cord.

To make the mold, we used modeling clay available at craft and toy stores. Press a pattern into the clay with a blunt paintbrush handle or something similar. Here the jewelry is shaped like a flower.

Insert a toothpick into the clay where you want the hole for threading the ribbon. Fill the mold with concrete.

The result is a decorative concrete flower to wear around your neck.

A beautiful concrete tray can be used both indoors and out. It sits pretty on the garden table, is useful for planting in the flowerbeds, or makes a handy tray for putting out vegetables in the kitchen.

A WONDERFUL *Tray*

For this tray, crocheted cloths come in handy again. We cut them in several, seperate pieces in order to create a unique pattern. Two cheap aluminum platters from the grocery store served as the mold. With a dollop of concrete in between them, our tray was done!

- Brush the inside of one platter with vegetable oil.
- Cut the crocheted cloth into pieces.
- Place the other tray upside down and arrange the fabric pieces on top. Brush them with oil.
- Mix the concrete as described on page 12.
- Spread the concrete so that it covers the platter and the cloths entirely. Press the other platter on top. This makes the surface smooth on both the inside and outside.
- Weigh the top platter down with rocks so everything stays in place.
- Allow the tray to cure and dry for at least twenty-four hours. Don't place it in direct sunlight.
- Remove the weights, remove the tray from the mold, and remove the cloths.
- The tray is done!

Brush the surface thoroughly with vegetable oil.

Place the cloths on the platter in whatever pattern you choose.

Pour the concrete over both the tray and the fabric. Spread it in an even layer, about ½ to ¾ of an inch (1–2 cm) thick, so that the platter is completely covered.

" Being creative is most enjoyable when you successfully turn something you already have at home into something new. You save the environment—since nothing is wasted—and you save money because you don't need to buy anything new. Can it get any better? "

Cover with the second tray so the surface of the finished tray becomes smooth on both the inside and the outside.

Add weights so the tray stays in place. Stones work just fine.

Hand IN A GLOVE

This concrete piece may be purely decorative, but it's easy and fun to make. Fill a plastic glove with concrete, and you'll have a helping hand to place around the home—a good project to do with the kids!

- Mix the concrete as described on page 12.
- Pour the concrete into the glove.
- Hang the glove to dry and let it cure for at least twenty-four hours. Don't place it in direct sunlight.
- Carefully pull the glove off the hand.

Use a regular plastic glove as the mold, and fill it up with concrete. Hang it to dry.

A smooth hand made of concrete looks pretty funny.

Candy Bowl

This simple little bowl has been cast in a toilet brush holder (newly purchased, of course!). You have to use a little imagination to find new, interesting shapes! The cradle becomes a perfect mold when it's turned upside down.

- Turn the holder upside down and brush the inside with vegetable oil.
- Mix the concrete as described on page 12.
- Pour the concrete into the mold.
- Gently tap it against the ground a few times to remove any air bubbles.
- Let the bowl cure and dry for at least twenty-four hours. Don't place it in direct sunlight.
- For best results, spray the concrete with water a few times during the drying period.
- Carefully remove the bowl from the mold. You'll probably need to be patient and coax it a little.
- The bowl is now ready to be filled with tasty treats.

A new toilet brush holder is the mold for the bowl.

Brush the inside with vegetable oil.

Fill the mold with concrete, smooth the edges, and gently tap against the ground to remove any air bubbles.

Look how luscious the little bowl turned out. Fill it with something tasty!

Grouped CANDLEHOLDERS

It always looks cozy to see tealights in candleholders—and grouping them together makes the greatest impact. Here we've connected several candleholders to make one large one. As we've said, when searching for shapes you have to let your imagination go wild. For this project, we used a container that's made to hold fresh plants. Ask for them at the nursery or grocery store and you can probably get a couple.

- Brush the inside of the mold with vegetable oil.
- Mix the concrete as described on page 12.
- Pour the concrete into the mold, but don't fill it completely. You'll need to leave space for the tealights.
- Press the desired number of tealights into the wet concrete.
- Gently tap the mold against the ground a few times to remove any air bubbles.
- Let the candleholders cure and dry for at least twenty-four hours. Don't place them in direct sunlight.
- For best results, spray the concrete with water a few times during the drying period.
- Carefully remove the tealights from the plastic mold.
- Light the candles and enjoy!

" Not all stores can offer unique items for great prices. When it comes to finding molds for concrete casting, the flea market is unbeatable. Keep your eyes and imagination open as you shop, and ask yourself 'Can I turn this upside done and pour concrete into it?' "

The mold was an old, plastic plant holder from the grocery store. Before, there were fresh flowers in it. Now it's the perfect candleholder.

Pour the concrete into the mold, but remember to leave room for the tealights.

Press the desired number of tealights into the wet concrete.

A personal and creative candleholder to show off with pride.

Patio UMBRELLA BASE

A patio umbrella base should be really heavy, which makes concrete the perfect material. It can be difficult to find an attractive base at the store, so we'll show you how to cast one yourself.

- Start with the shape of the particle board. Saw a bottom and four side panels. We made our parasol base in a square shape.
- Nail the pieces together into a box.
- Cut a strip of wood, and nail it to the inside of the box at the preferred height. This will make a stylish edge at the top of the base.
- Tie a long rope into two loops. These will stick out from the concrete. Place the rope in the box. The loops will act as handles.
- Mix the concrete as described on page 12.
- Pour the concrete. Fill the box up to the wooden strip, and smooth the surface.
- Insert a plastic tube into the concrete, in the middle of the box. We used a piece of sewer pipe. This is where you will insert the umbrella.
- Ensure that the rope loops are correctly placed.
- Decorate with beautiful stones.
- Let the base cure and dry for at least twenty-four hours. Don't place it in direct sunlight.
- For best results, spray the concrete with water a few times during the drying period.
- Remove the parasol base from the mold.

Nail the particle board together to form a box.

Form the rope into two loops. They will come up from the sides to serve as handles. Pour concrete up to the strip of wood.

Insert the plastic tube into the wet concrete. We used a piece of sewer pipe.

Once the stones are pressed into the wet concrete, it's now ready to cure and dry.

The heavy base holds the patio umbrella securely in place.

Concrete Medallions

Elegant concrete medallions are nice to have both inside the house and out. For one medallion, we created the pattern with a potholder, and for the other, we used a ceiling rose made of Styrofoam.

- To make the first tray, we used two round pie tins in different sizes and a crocheted potholder.
- Brush the potholder with oil on both sides.
- Place the smaller pie tin upside down, brush with oil, and lay the oiled potholder on top.
- Brush the inside of the larger tin with oil.
- Mix the concrete as described on page 12.
- Spread the concrete so that it covers the mold and potholder completely, and then place the larger pie tin on top. This allows you to create a smooth surface on both sides of the medallion. Press down and smooth the edges.
- Cover with a weight so the shape stays in place.
- Let the medallion cure and dry for at least twenty-four hours. Don't place it in direct sunlight.
- Remove the weights and separate the medallion from the molds.

- To make the second tray, use a ceiling rose made of Styrofoam. You can find these in well-stocked home improvement stores. Start by brushing the ceiling rose with oil.
- Cover the rose completely with the mixed concrete. Smooth the surface and edges.
- Spray the concrete with water a few times during the drying period.
- Remove the medallion from the Styrofoam.
- Done!

Medallions can be made two ways. These were made with different sized pie tins and a potholder.

Two elegant concrete medallions, ready to use.

The ceiling rose's pattern is clearly visible in the medallion.

A ceiling rose made of Styrofoam
can be found at home improvement
stores. Brush the top with
vegetable oil.

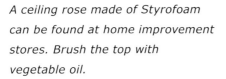

Cover the entire piece of ceiling
stucco with concrete. Smooth
the edges and surface.

Birdbath WITH SCULPTED LEAVES

You can never have too many birdbaths. They're beautiful in the garden, on the patio, or on the balcony. This birdbath got an extra touch with small concrete leaves for decoration.

- CONCRETE LEAVES can be made in the same way as the Rhubarb Leaf Fruit Bowl on page 14, but you can use the small leaves of any plant. Choose ones with a beautiful shape and distinct veins. The small concrete leaves should be completely finished before you start with the birdbath, as this project is done in two stages.

- FOR THE BIRDBATH we used a round plastic tub and a small plastic bowl with a round shape.
- Brush the inside of the large tub and the outside of the small bowl with vegetable oil.
- Mix the concrete as described on page 12.
- Pour the concrete into the large tub. Don't fill it completely; leave room for the other bowl.
- Press the small bowl into the wet concrete.
- Gently tap the mold against the ground a few times to remove any air bubbles.
- Fill the smaller bowl with a few large stones to keep it in place.
- Place the finished concrete leaves where you like.
- Let the birdbath cure and dry for at least twenty-four hours. Don't place it in direct sunlight.
- For best results, spray the concrete with water a few times during the drying period.
- Remove the weights and loosen the two molds from the concrete.
- Pour water into the bath, and maybe add some fresh-cut flowers.
- Set the bath outside for the birds, or let the bowl serve as a cute addition to your garden or balcony.

Here, the smaller bowl has been pressed into the concrete and a weight added to keep the bowl's shape. The leaves have been set in place, and the bath will cure for at least twenty-four hours.

The decorative birdbath in place in the garden.

Polka Dot FLOWERPOT

Pots can be made an infinite number of ways, and you can vary both their shapes and sizes. This flowerpot has a polka dot pattern made by using a piece of rubber flooring.

- We used a plastic bucket and a large sour cream container.
- To make the polka dot pattern on the outside, we lined the bucket with a piece of dot-patterned rubber flooring. Skip this step if you'd prefer a plain surface.
- Brush the inside of the bucket and flooring, and the outside of the sour cream container, with vegetable oil.
- Mix the concrete as described on page 12.
- Pour the concrete into the bucket, but leave room for the sour cream container.
- Press down the plastic container.
- Gently tap the bucket against the ground a few times to remove any air bubbles.
- Cover with weights.
- Let your pot cure and dry for at least twenty-four hours. Don't place it in direct sunlight.
- For best results, spray the concrete with water a few times during the drying period.
- Remove the weights and remove the pot from the molds.
- Plant a flower in the flowerpot and enjoy your creation.

Below is everything we used to make a flowerpot that's a little different: a bucket, a piece of flooring, and a large container that used to hold sour cream . . .

*See how beautifully it
turned out? It looks
very professional!*

Bottle Bookend

Isn't our bookend cool? We cast it in an old fabric softener bottle. This is yet another example of how old packaging is perfectly suited for use as molds.

- Unscrew the cap on the bottle and cut a hole in the top.
- Mix the concrete as described on page 12.
- Fill the bottle with concrete.
- Replace the cap and pour concrete through the hole you made.
- Gently tap the bottle against the ground to remove any air bubbles.
- Let the bookend cure and dry for at least twenty-four hours. Don't place it in direct sunlight.
- Unscrew the cap and cut open the bottle to release the bookend.

The bottle should be filled all the way up to the edge with concrete.

When the lid you've cut open is screwed back on, you can fill that up with concrete too.

A heavy, sturdy, and good-looking bookend made of concrete.

BLOSSOMING *Garden Ornament*

We've made a really luscious garden ornament from a plastic mold we found at a flea market. It was actually meant as a wall decoration, but if you turn it upside down, it's the perfect shape to fill with concrete.

- Brush the inside of the mold with vegetable oil.
- Mix the concrete as described on page 12.
- Fill the mold with concrete.
- Spread the concrete so the surface is smooth.
- Gently tap the mold against the ground a few times to remove any air bubbles.
- Allow the ornament to cure and dry for at least twenty-four hours. Don't place it in direct sunlight.
- For best results, spray the concrete with water a few times during the drying period.
- Carefully remove the ornament from the mold by bending it gently.
- The ornament is ready for the garden plot or wherever you want a lovely decoration.

Fill the mold with concrete.

Even out the concrete so the surface is smooth.

The blossoming ornament is finished; stylish enough to display outside in the garden or anywhere you want it!

Bench WITH A PATTERNED EDGE

A classic concrete bench is a useful piece of furniture in the garden. Of course you can sit on it, but it also looks nice with flowerpots on top. The table is cast in a mold of particle board and reinforced with chicken wire. The countertop is then laid on a pile of bricks at the desired height. To create the pattern on the side, we used a strip of Styrofoam edging. You can find these at well-stocked home improvement stores.

- Build the mold from particle board and a formwork.
- Measure and screw the formwork into the desired shape.
- Screw the formwork onto the particle board.
- Cut the chicken wire to fit the mold.
- Add the Styrofoam strips along the long sides.
- Mix the concrete as described on page 12.
- Fill the mold with concrete.
- Press the reinforcement—chicken wire—into the concrete.
- Gently tap the mold against the ground a few times to remove any air bubbles.
- Let the bench cure and dry for at least twenty-four hours. Don't place it in direct sunlight.
- For best results, spray the concrete with water a few times during the drying period.
- Carefully free the solid bench top by bending the mold slightly.
- The bench top is ready to be used.

The mold consists of particle board and a standard formwork. Measure and screw the formwork into the desired shape, then screw it onto the particle board. Cut the chicken wire to fit the mold and add Styrofoam edging along the length of the bench.

Have a seat! This small bench top was placed on top of two piles of bricks, and the bench is complete.

Strips of Styrofoam edging give the sides of the bench a beautiful pattern.

PATTERNED *Slab*

You can make a robust and decorative concrete slab with a pretty pattern by using a plastic storage bin and a rubber doormat. The slab should be reinforced so it doesn't break. Use it as a step or simply as a decoration.

- Brush the doormat and the inside of the storage bin with vegetable oil.
- Place the doormat in the bottom of the bin. You can get this type of doormat from your local hardware store.
- Cut the chicken wire to the appropriate size, for reinforcement.
- Mix the concrete as described on page 12.
- Pour concrete into the bin so that it completely covers the doormat. The height and thickness should each be about 2 inches (5 cm).
- Press the chicken wire into the concrete and smooth the surface.
- Gently tap the mold a few times to remove any air bubbles.
- Allow the slab to cure and dry for at least twenty-four hours. Don't place it in direct sunlight.
- For best results, spray the concrete with water a few times during the drying period.
- Remove the slab from the mold and carefully pull the doormat from the slab.
- The pretty slab is now ready for use.

" Concrete is not a perishable item, so you can keep a bag lying around in the garage until you get the chance to use it. Make sure it's not damp, as it easily absorbs moisture and will eventually solidify. "

A white plastic storage bin from Ikea fit
the dimensions of the doormat perfectly.

Pour the concrete into the bin so that
it covers the doormat completely.
The height and thickness should each
be about 2 inches (5 cm).

Smooth the surface with a shovel;
this will be the underside of the slab.

The concrete slabs are ready.
Here they serve as a steps.

The doormat gave the slab its
beautiful pattern.

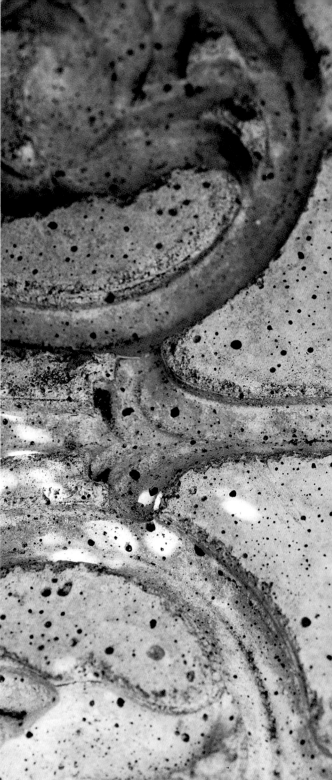

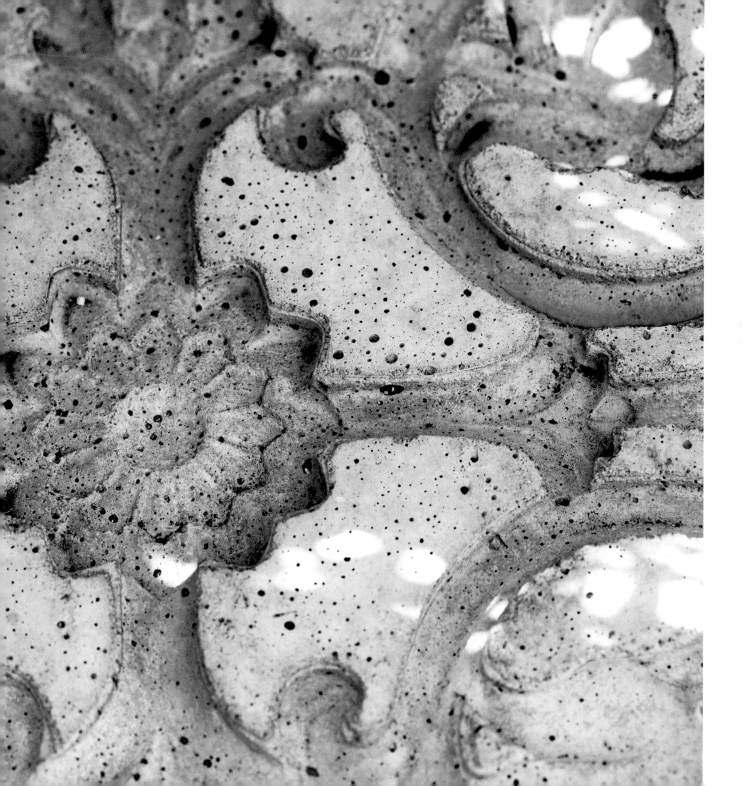

THREEFOLD *Birdbath*

As we said, you can't have too many birdbaths! For this, we used a threefold plastic bowl to give the birdbath a beautiful and unique shape.

- We used a large plastic tub and a smaller, threefold bowl with round compartments.
- Brush the inside of the tub and the outside of the bowl with vegetable oil.
- Mix the concrete as described on page 12.
- Pour the concrete into the tub, but don't fill it completely. Save room for the other bowl.
- Push the small bowl into the wet concrete.
- Gently tap the mold against the ground a few times to remove any air bubbles.
- Add a few large stones to keep the upper bowl in place.
- Let the birdbath cure for at least twenty-four hours. Don't place it in direct sunlight.
- For best results, spray the concrete with water a few times during the drying period.
- Remove the weights and take the birdbath from the mold.
- Fill the birdbath with water, and maybe add a few cut flowers.
- Set out in the garden for the birds.

A tub and a plastic bowl of different shapes and sizes are the perfect molds for the birdbath.

Brush the inside of the bucket and the outside of the bowl with vegetable oil.

Pour concrete into the bucket and press the bowl down into the wet concrete.

Place some heavy stones in the bowl to hold it in place. Let it cure for at least twenty-four hours.

This beautiful birdbath is ready to be placed in the garden.

LACE-PATTERNED *Trivet*

An easy and simple project to tackle that's also very useful! Concrete is an excellent material to use for trivets, and this pattern was made using a crochet lace doily.

- Use a round shape with a flat bottom like a large sour cream container. If you want a square trivet, use a large square-shaped plastic container.
- Brush the inside of the mold with vegetable oil.
- Place a crochet lace doily on the bottom and brush it with vegetable oil.
- Mix the concrete as described on page 12.
- Pour the concrete into the mold so that the concrete is approximately 1 inch (2½ cm) thick.
- Gently tap the mold against the ground a few times to remove any air bubbles.
- Let the trivet cure and dry for at least twenty-four hours. Don't place it in direct sunlight.
- For best results, spray the concrete with water a few times during the drying period.
- Remove the trivet from the mold.
- Line the bottom with felt pads. The concrete can be rough and might scratch the table surface of it's not padded.

A charming trivet for the coffee pot, pan, or casserole dish.

Dresser WITH A CONCRETE TOP

We made this charming old dresser that we purchased at a flea market for fifteen dollars even more charming when we topped it with this concrete slab. Decorating it with some molded tiles was the icing on the cake. Start by building a mold, and to make the slab sturdy, reinforce it with chicken wire.

- The mold is made from particle board and a standard formwork purchased at a lumberyard. Measure and screw the formwork to the desired size.
- Screw the formwork onto the particle board.
- Cut the chicken wire to a size that fits the mold.
- Mix concrete as described on page 12.
- Place tiles in the mold with the bottoms facing upward.
- Fill mold with concrete.
- Press the chicken wire into the concrete for reinforcement.
- Gently tap the mold against the ground a few times to remove any air bubbles.
- Let the slab cure and dry for at least twenty-four hours. Don't place it in direct sunlight.
- For best results, spray the concrete with water a few times during the drying period.
- Loosen the slab gently from the mold by bending the mold slightly.
- Place the slab on top of the dresser. The slab is heavy enough that it doesn't have to be attached with screws.

Decorative tiles will liven up the concrete dresser top.

❝ *The once dull dresser looks trendy with the new concrete top. Cast the slab and put it on the dresser—done! Now place your dresser somewhere in the spotlight!* ❞

Screw the formwork onto the particle board and place the tiles upside down.

Doesn't the concrete gray contrast nicely with the bright green tiles? Ask at a tile store for leftover tiles.

The slab gives the dresser a new look, and the surface area on top of the dresser is now larger.

Cozy Candleholders

Instead of recycling plastic bottles, use them as candlestick molds! Look at the bottom of the bottle and see what a nice shape it has.

- Cut the bottles, and keep only the bottom. We left about 4 inches (10 cm) in height.
- Brush the inside of the bottles with vegetable oil.
- Mix the concrete as described on page 12.
- Fill the bottle-bottoms most of the way with concrete.
- Gently tap the bottles against the ground a few times to remove any air bubbles.
- Insert a taper candle into the concrete—make sure it stands securely.
- Let the candlesticks cure and dry for at least twenty-four hours. Don't place them in direct sunlight.
- For best results, spray the concrete with water a few times during the drying period.
- Loosen the candlesticks from the bottles. You may need to cut the plastic off.
- Set the candlesticks in a group and light them up!

A different kind of recycling! A couple of plastic bottles make perfect candlestick molds.

Cut the bottles and only keep the bottom part. Ours are about four inches (10 cm) high.

Fill the cut bottles with concrete almost up to the edge, and insert the candles.

Three concrete candlesticks fit nicely on the windowsill.

Mirror, Mirror

To make a mirror frame from concrete, build a mold from a formwork and particle board. Screw the parts together into a frame and fill it with concrete. Attach cardboard patterns to the particle board to decorate the concrete. The mirror frame needs to be reinforced so it won't break. Since the mirror is quite heavy, we recommend leaning it against the wall rather than hanging it up. It will look great on top of the cabinet in the hallway, for example.

- The mold is made from particle board and a formwork purchased from the lumberyard.
- Measure and screw the formwork into one larger and one smaller square. The width of the frame is made from the difference in size.
- Measure carefully and screw the formwork onto the particle board.
- Glue the cardboard pattern (available at your local craft store) on the particle board so that it stays in place.
- For reinforcement, cut chicken wire to fit in the frame.
- Mix the concrete as described on page 12.
- Fill the mold between the formwork with concrete.
- Press the chicken wire into the concrete.
- Gently tap the mold against the ground a few times to remove any air bubbles.
- If you choose, you can cast in metal hooks for hanging.
- Let the framework cure and dry for at least twenty-four hours. Don't place it in direct sunlight.
- For best results, spray the concrete with water a few times during the drying period.
- Carefully remove the framework from the mirror by bending the formwork slightly.
- Remove the cardboard pattern.
- Glue on the mirror glass with an adhesive that sticks to glass and concrete.

First, screw the formwork into two squares—one larger and one smaller. Measure carefully, and screw them onto the particle board. The concrete is poured between the two squares—not in the middle, where the mirror glass will sit.

If you want to decorate the frame, glue a cardboard pattern onto the particle board. It will create a design in the concrete.

Our mirror leaning against the wall in the greenhouse will be a nice interior decoration.

The Black Pot

If you want your concrete project to be a different color than the original gray, paint it! The concrete must be thoroughly dry before it can be painted. You can use many different kinds of paint, such as floor paint suitable for concrete floors. Ask at the paint store which type is most suitable. Water-based paints get absorbed into the concrete and create a glazed appearance, while lacquers sit on top of the surface. For our black pot, we used a black varnish stain, and the result was a beautiful, gray-black hue with a gradient effect.

- Start by casting a pot using a large plastic bucket and either a smaller one or a plastic container. We used a bucket and a big sour cream container.
- Brush the inside of the large bucket and the outside of the smaller container with vegetable oil.
- Mix the concrete as described on page 12.
- Pour the concrete into the bucket, but don't fill it completely, so there's room for the smaller container inside.
- Press down on the container.
- Gently tap the bucket against the ground a few times to remove any air bubbles.
- Add weights to keep the smaller container in place; stones work perfectly.
- Let the pot cure and dry for at least twenty-four hours. Don't place it in direct sunlight.
- For best results, spray the concrete with water a few times during the drying period.
- Remove the weights and loosen the pot from the container and bucket.
- Paint the pot once or several times.

We painted the pot once with a black varnish stain and thought it looked very pretty.

The painted pot has a beautiful, gray-black color with a gradient effect.

Beautiful shapes with beautiful textures.

A BEAUTIFUL *Decoration*

Our imaginations ran wild! We created a mold out of Styrofoam and filled it with concrete. We had no idea what the result would be, but when the concrete cured and the Styrofoam was removed, we thought that the sculpture—with its soft shape in the hard concrete—was really cool.

- You need a large Styrofoam sheet about 4 inches (10 cm) thick and regular particle board. You can find both at the home improvement store.
- Draw the pattern on the Styrofoam.
- Cut out the pattern with a scalpel or knife.
- Screw the Styrofoam onto the particle board so it stays in place.
- Mix the concrete as described on page 12.
- Pour the concrete into the pattern.
- Allow the concrete to cure and dry for at least twenty-four hours. Don't place it in direct sunlight.
- For best results, spray the concrete with water a few times during the drying period.
- Loosen the particle board and remove the Styrofoam.
- Now you have a beautiful decoration!

" Often, we'll gather together a group of friends for an afternoon of concrete casting—we craft, socialize, eat, and have lots of fun together. Everyone contributes something—ideas and materials—to our concrete potluck. We highly recommend it! "

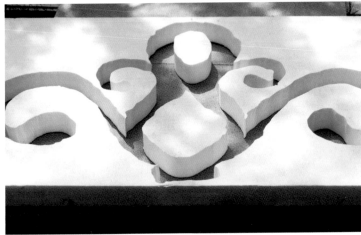

Draw a pattern by hand directly onto the Styrofoam sheet.

Cut the pattern and lay the Styrofoam on top of the particle board. This will serve as the bottom of the mold.

Fill the pattern with concrete.

Timeless CANDELABRA

This candelabra was cast in a box made from a few wooden planks and a small piece of particle board. The pattern was made using a piece of Styrofoam edging and four candleholders placed in the bottom. The candelabra can be decorated according to the season—flowers or pine sprigs pair beautifully with the concrete.

- Cut the planks and the particle board pieces to the desired size.
- Screw the parts into a box.
- Put the Styrofoam edging in the bottom along both long sides. You can find Styrofoam edgings at the home improvement store.
- Glue the four candleholders (available at your local craft store) upside down in the bottom of the mold.
- Mix the concrete as described on page 12.
- Fill the mold with concrete.
- Gently tap the mold against the ground a few times to remove any air bubbles.
- Allow the concrete to cure and dry for at least twenty-four hours. Don't place it in direct sunlight.
- Gently loosen the candleholder from the mold.
- Attach some felt pads on the bottom, because unprotected concrete is rough and can scratch surfaces.
- Decorate with flowers, twigs, or anything else you like.

The mold is ready to be filled with concrete.

The candelabra is absolutely adorable on the summer table with some cut flowers.

The pretty pattern is created by using a strip of Styrofoam edging. You can find these at the home improvement store.

To avoid scratching the surface of the table, it's good to put felt pads on the underside of the candelabra.

" If you keep a bag of concrete powder handy at home, it's easy to make something spontaneously. "

At Christmas use it as an Advent candelabra.

Concrete Cherub

This little concrete cherub was cast from a soap mold. It's a good example of using molds that were intended for purposes other than concrete casting. The cherub makes a cute little paperweight.

- Brush the inside of the mold (available at your local craft store) with vegetable oil.
- Mix the concrete as described on page 12.
- Fill the mold with concrete.
- Gently tap the mold against the ground to remove any air bubbles.
- Let the cherub cure and dry for at least twenty-four hours. Don't place it in direct sunlight.
- For best results, spray the concrete with water a few times during the drying period.
- Carefully loosen the cherub from the mold.

The concrete cherub keeps loose napkins or papers in place. If you make more, they can be placed on the tablecloth during outdoor parties, so it doesn't flutter away in the breeze.

Casting CONCRETE STEPS

A mold for casting concrete steps is as easy to make as the steps are useful. One step was missing at our greenhouse, so we cast one right on the spot and decorated it with pretty stones.

- Excavate the soil where the step is to be placed, and make sure the surface is even.
- Screw together three boards to make a frame. Use four if the step isn't going to be placed directly against the wall.
- Place the frame where the step will be cast.
- Fill the frame with gravel, shingle, or rocks so it doesn't use as much concrete.
- Use chicken wire as reinforcement and cut it so it fits in the frame.
- Mix the concrete as described on page 12.
- Pour the concrete into the frame and smooth the surface with a trowel or something similar.
- Press the chicken wire into the concrete and cover with more concrete, if needed.
- If you would like to decorate the step, press some stones, or whatever you choose, down into the concrete.
- Let the step cure and dry for at least twenty-four hours. Keep it in the shade as much as possible—you might need to shade it with an umbrella.
- For best results, spray the concrete with water a few times during the drying period.
- Remove the frame, and the step is done!

When the surface is nice and even, screw three planks together to make a frame and place it on the ground.

Fill the frame with gravel or rocks so you don't need to mix a lot of concrete.

The concrete is in place, and now it will cure.

A stylish and strong surface to step on!

BARBECUE *Station*

When summer and barbecue time arrives, it's nice to have a big barbecue with a roomy work surface. We rescued an old table our neighbors were going to throw away, and it became the starting point for our barbecue station. The appearance of the station varies depending on the base you choose, but the principle is the same. Build a mold from a formwork and particle board, place the barbecue bowl inside, add the concrete, and reinforce the slab—later the slab can be placed on any base of your choice.

- The mold is made of particle board and a formwork from the lumberyard.
- The grill is a regular kettle barbecue with a lid (but without the base) from your local home improvement store.
- Measure and screw the formwork into the desired shape.
- Place the grill bottom upside down, without the lid, at the desired position on the particle board.
- Cut the chicken wire to the dimensions that will fit into the mold and grill.
- Screw the formwork onto the particle board.
- Put a strip of silicone around the edge of the grill so the concrete can't escape, and put a pair of heavy stones on top of the grill to keep it stable during the process.
- Mix the concrete as described on page 12.
- Pour the concrete into the mold.
- Press the chicken wire into the concrete.
- Gently tap the mold against the ground a few times to remove any air bubbles.
- Let the slab cure and dry for at least twenty-four hours. Don't place it in direct sunlight.
- For best results, spray the concrete with water a few times during the drying period.
- Remove the slab from the mold by gently bending the mold a little.
- Attach the slab to the station; it's so heavy that it can just be placed on top. Place the cooking grate and lid on the grill.

Our starting point for the barbecue station was this table in two levels. We poured two slabs, but only one with the barbecue.

Lay down the particle board and measure where to put the barbecue. Then, put a strip of silicone around the edge of the grill, and place the grill upside down on the particle board (without the lid).

Finish the mold by screwing the formwork onto the particle board.

Fill the mold with concrete and reinforce it with chicken wire. Place some stones on the grill so it stays in place.

Smooth the surface thoroughly.

Now let the concrete cure for at least twenty-four hours.

The grill is cast in the concrete, and the slab provides a roomy workspace.

Both concrete slabs are in place, and the barbecue station is installed in the garden. It's time to start grilling!

We stained the base in black to match the grill. Don't you think it's a stylish piece of patio furniture?

TREATING THE *Concrete*

There are several ways to treat the concrete to give it various textures and appearances. Experiment with it to get new results; it's both interesting and educational, and you'll probably make some new discoveries.

VARNISH Boat varnish gives the concrete a glossy surface. It's important that the concrete be completely dry before varnishing. If any water remains, it's likely to form bubbles. Let any concrete project rest a couple of weeks prior to coating it.

DRILL HOLES Drilling into concrete tends to be associated with difficult situations, such as placing a shelf on a concrete wall, and the drill can hardly cope. But for such projects that are thinner and smaller, a regular drill will work just fine for making holes.

SMOOTH Sharp edges on concrete are easy to smooth down with ordinary sandpaper. If you have, for example, a table or a bench with sharp edges, it's advisable to smooth them down slightly, so they get a rounder shape that's more attractive and less painful to bump into!

The edge is jagged and very sharp.

Smooth with ordinary sandpaper to give the concrete a softer edge.

For projects that are thin, it's easy to use a regular drill to make holes. The blossoming garden ornament could be the start of a fountain, now that it has a hole in the middle.

SOAP By using a soap designed to be used on stone, the concrete will be saturated and protected by the detergent. This is good for objects that are left outdoors.

WAX Wax (for stone) and paraffin oil protect against stains and give the concrete surface a nice luster. Rub the wax or oil in properly.

PAINT You can use many different kinds of paints on concrete. A water-based paint gets absorbed into the concrete and gives a more stained impression, while lacquers coat the surface.